CANADA, MY LAND

CANADA, MY LAND

WILLIAM MACKAY MACKERACHER

ISBN: 978-93-5614-611-2

Published: 1908

LECTOR HOUSE

LECTOR HOUSE LLP
E-MAIL: info@lectorhouse.com

CANADA, MY LAND
AND OTHER COMPOSITIONS IN VERSE

BY

W. M. MACKERACHER

1908

CONTENTS

CANADA, MY LAND.

There may be more enchanting climes

There may be more enchanting climes
Within a southern zone;
There may be eastern Edens deckt
With charms to thee unknown;
But thou art fairest unto me,
Because thou art mine own,
Canada, my land.

More spacious plains and loftier heights
In other realms may be,
And mightier streams than those which bear
Thy waters to the sea;
But thou, great handiwork of God,
Art grandest unto me,
Canada, my land.

More glorious records may adorn
The annals of the past
Than those which tell the rise and growth
Of thy dominion vast;
But I am proudest of the land
In which my lot is cast,
Canada, my land.

Beneath thy green or snow-clad sod
My fathers' ashes lie;
Thou hast my all, to thee I'm bound
By every dearest tie;
For thee I'll gladly live, for thee
I cheerfully would die,
Canada, my land.

FORWARD, CANADA!

Northland of our birth and rearing

Northland of our birth and rearing,
Bound to us by ties endearing,—
Forward ever, nothing fearing!
Forward, Canada!

Hear thy children's acclamations!
Vanquish trials and vexations!
Higher rise among the nations!
Forward, Canada!

Not by battles fierce and gory,
Not by conquest's hollow glory,
Need'st thou live in deathless story:
Forward, Canada!

Not by might and not by power,—-
Truth shall be thy fortress tower;
Arts of peace shall be thy flower:
Forward, Canada!

Yet if tyrant foe should ever
'Gainst thee come with base endeavor,
Strike, and yield thy freedom never:
Forward, Canada!

CANADIAN-BORN.

Although I'm not unduly proud

Although I'm not unduly proud,
Inordinately vain,
But humble, as will be allowed,
And modest in the main;
I must confess to pride of birth,
And all detractors warn
To let alone one land on earth:
I am Canadian-born.

In one respect I fill the bill
As well as any man
Between Vancouver and Brazil,
Morocco and Japan.
From Hobart Town to Hammerfest,
From Greenland to the Horn,
My native land is much the best:
I am Canadian-born.

The Greeks beside their Hellespont
Thought all but they were scum;
The Latins loved the classic vaunt,
"Civis Romanus sum."
I'm not so impudent as they
To hold the world in scorn,
But have a better boast to-day,
"I am Canadian-born."

My land is beauty's flag unfurled,
A garden of increase,
The crowning wonder of the world,
Creation's masterpiece;
And deathless deed and kingly name
Her chronicles adorn;
I'm pardonably proud to claim
I am Canadian-born.

I love her cities old and new,
Her crested mountain-chains,

Her lakes and rivers fair to view,
Her meadows and her plains,
Her tented fields of yellow sheaves,
Her spears of towering corn,
Her forests with their maple leaves:
I am Canadian-born.

I love her verdant springtime sweet,
Her autumn red and gold;
I love her summer's tropic heat,
Her winter's arctic cold,
The splendor of her evening glow,
The glory of her morn;
And day and night I love to know
I am Canadian-born.

All honor to her pioneers,
The gallant sons of France;
All honor to their British peers,
Who aided her advance;
To workers like the great Champlain,
And Dufferin and Lorne,
And those who could take up the strain,
"I am Canadian-born."

Here my allotted time I'd live
And play my little part,
My service here to Nature give,
To Industry and Art;
Here pluck life's roses when I may,
And when I feel the thorn
Look up with fortitude and say,
"I am Canadian-born."

And should unfriendly circumstance
(Which Providence forbid!)
Decree that from my latest glance
My country should be hid,
Ah, then 'twill ease my parting sigh
And cheer my heart forlorn,
To think, wherever I may die,
I am Canadian-born.

KNOW'ST THOU THE LAND?

Know'st thou the land where the pious and bold

Know'st thou the land where the pious and bold
Beared Christianity's emblem of old,
And civilization's beneficent reign
Extended o'er anarchy's savage domain?
The land of the dauntless explorers who prest
Upstream, through the wilderness, into the West?
Know'st thou the land of the soldier and knight,
The land of adventure and toil and delight?
Know'st thou the land?
Know'st thou the land?
'Tis the land of my home, my beloved native land.

Know'st thou the land where the Briton and Gaul,
In courage and prowess supreme over all,
Contending for lordship and vying for place,
Collided and locked in a mighty embrace
So bravely that fame has awarded the palm
Of deathless renown to both Wolfe and Montcalm?
Know'st thou the land for which heroes have died,
The land of the strong and the true and the tried?

Know'st thou the land of the broad maple tree?
The noblest and best of his fellows is he:
He grows in the meadow, the grove and the wood;
His trunk is for timber, his sap is for food;
His boughs are for fire in the cold winter days;
His leaves are for shade from the summer sun's blaze.
Know'st thou the land of the maple benign,
The land of the elm and the oak and the pine?

Know'st thou the land where the great inland seas
Are tossed by the tempest or fanned by the breeze;
The land of Superior's crystalline tide,
Of Huron's exuberant vigor and pride,
Of Erie's alluring voluptuous glance,
Ontario's laughing Elysian expanse?
Know'st thou the land that is praised evermore
By the chant of their surge and Niagara's roar?

Know'st thou the land of the clear-flowing streams
That mirror the stars and reflect the sun's beams?
Through the woods and the farmland they wander at large,
And the deer and the kine come to drink at their marge;
They flash in the distance like ribands of white;
Their trout-haunted pools are the angler's delight.
Know'st thou the land of the rivers and rills,
The boon of the lowlands, the joy of the hills?

Know'st thou the land where St. Lawrence proceeds
By cities and hamlets and blossoming meads
And islands and waters of lesser degree,
With his tribute to pour in the lap of the sea?
His shining battalions he halts to deploy,
Or leaps through the rapid with turbulent joy.
Know'st thou the land that he laves in his flow,
Where deep-laden argosies royally go?

Know'st thou the land of the mountains that rise
Till their summits are lost in the depths of the skies?
Their granite foundations are far underground,
Where the gold and the coal and the iron abound;
And the sun on their white-headed majesty flings
The radiance of crowns and the purple of kings.
Know'st thou the land of these citadels tall,
With their ramparts and battlements, wall upon wall?

Know'st thou the land where the ice and the snow
On all things a magical beauty bestow?
Then the earth is a bride and the tingling air wine,
The frosty sky sparkles, the Pleiades shine,
And the bright "merry dancers" in gorgeous array,
Like ghosts of dead sunbeams, come forth to their play.
Know'st thou the land of the sleigh-bells, the land
Of the warm fireside and the welcoming hand?

Know'st thou the land where kind Nature has given
In earth's beauty and grandeur a foretaste of heaven;
Where History lingers, enthralled with the view
Of as splendid exploits as the world ever knew;
Where Industry reaps the rewards of her toil
In the wealth of the cities, the fruits of the soil?
Know'st thou the land which the Muses regard,
The land of the sculptor, the singer, the bard?

Know'st thou the land where the spell of the past
Is over the mind irresistibly cast;
Where the present fulfills the fond hopes of the years,
The dreams of romancers, the visions of seers,

Where the future inspires with a prospect sublime,
Maturing the fairest fruition of time?
Know'st thou this land of Heaven's favor possest,
The fortunate land of a destiny blest?
Know'st thou the land?
Know'st thou the land?
'Tis the land of my home, my belov'd native land.

O MAPLE LEAF!

Thee best of leaves I love

Thee best of leaves I love,
In forest or in grove,
O Maple Leaf;
O thou which art the sign
Of this dear land of mine,
What loveliness is thine,
O Maple Leaf!

Naught can with thee compare,
On earth or in the air,
O Maple Leaf;
Wondrous thy beauties are;
Thy form is like a star,
But thou art not afar,
O Maple Leaf.

When drops of dew adorn
Thy surface in the morn,
O Maple Leaf,
No hue so fair is seen,
In silk or satin's sheen,
As thy rich shade of green,
O Maple Leaf.

No music in my ear
Is half so sweet to hear,
O Maple Leaf,
As that which thou dost make
When winds of summer shake
The branches of the brake,
O Maple Leaf.

Most beautiful in pain,
When suns begin to wane,
O Maple Leaf,
Thou never growest old,
But in the time of cold
Thou turnest but to gold,

O Maple Leaf.

And when the earth expires,
And mute are all her choirs,
O Maple Leaf,
Thy dower thou dost shed
Of tribute, richest red,
Upon her sombre bed,
O Maple Leaf.

May heaven bless thy land,
And make it strong to stand,
O Maple Leaf;
For it we humbly pray
That God will be its stay,
Now, henceforth, and for aye,
O Maple Leaf.

DOMINION DAY.

Where the purple-vestured mountains

Where the purple-vestured mountains
Bear their summits crowned with snow,
Haughty lords of all the riches
In the rocks and streams below;
Tow'ring to the azure heavens,
Frowning on the sapphire sea:
There to-day, O wide Dominion,
Thine own children honor thee.

Where the shadeless, open prairie
Spreads its lone expanse unstirred
By a sound of living creature,
Save the lowing of the herd,
And the half-grown wheat in verdure
Reaches thickly to the knee,
There to-day, O fair Dominion,
Thine own children honor thee.

Where the south wind from the bushes
The large, luscious berry shakes,
And the commerce of the cities
Meets the traffic of the lakes,
And the thunderous Niag'ra
Sings the pæan of the free:
There to-day, O strong Dominion,
Thine own children honor thee.

Where the deep, majestic river
Bears upon its solemn tide,
By the haunts of ancient story
And the seats of former pride,
Ocean argosies to markets
Where the world is held in fee:
There to-day, O great Dominion,
Thine own children honor thee.

Where the stalwart sea-girt peoples
Keep the gateway of the land;

In the meadows of New Brunswick,
On the Nova Scotian strand,
In the Gulf's fair island garden,
Sheltered by the maple tree:
There to-day, O blest Dominion,
Thine own children honor thee.

In thy cherished mother country,
In thy sister lands afar,
On the burning eastern desert,
Underneath the southern star,
'Midst the speech of alien races,
Wheresoe'er thy children be,
There to-day, O dear Dominion,
Loyal hearts remember thee.

CANADA'S EIGHTEEN.

At Paardeberg they fell

At Paardeberg they fell,
Within the Orange State;
They did their duty well;
They bravely met their fate.

A stubborn fight they made
Upon the level plain,
While from the barricade
The bullets poured like rain.

They fiercely charged the trench;
They took the outer line;
Who saw a visage blench?
Who heard a voice repine?

They bore the ruthless fire;
But deadly was the cost:
They lived not to retire,
Nor saw their capture lost.

No lustrous deed they wrought
To prompt the epic pen:
They only bravely fought,
And gave their lives like men.

And yet no hero's fame
That rings across the seas,
Shall e'er eclipse the name
And memory of these.

While suns shall rise and set
Upon the fatal scene,
We never shall forget
Our Canada's Eighteen.

And now, as Britain weaves
The garland of her grief,
We place among the leaves
A blood-red maple leaf.

DOMINION DAY, 1900.

Rejoice, O Canada, rejoice

Rejoice, O Canada, rejoice,
On this thy natal day;
In East and West lift up thy voice,
And to thy children say:
"Behold me now to stature sprung;
Acclaim my second birth;
A Nation now I stand among
My sisters of the earth."

The wrath of man doth praise the Lord;
And, glorious be His name,
An Empire, fashioned by the sword
And welded in the flame,
Hath risen o'er the battle-smoke,
And near and far unfurled
Its righteous standard to evoke
Heaven's blessings on the world.

O CANADA, MON PAYS, MES AMOURS.

(Title of a French-Canadian song.)

O Canada, my country and my love

O Canada, my country and my love,
Held in my heart all other lands above;
To thee to whom my homage should belong
I pay the cheerful tribute of my song,
And swear allegiance as on bended knee,
And vow undying fealty to thee,
O Canada, my country and my love.

I crave no land of epic story cast
In giant shadows on the misty past;
No land illustrious in former time,
Which has outlived the vigor of its prime;
No lordlier land renowned across the sea,
Nor any other land on earth but thee,
O Canada, my country and my love.

Past is thy night of darkness and of tears;
Thy radiant dawn hath driv'n away our fears;
Thy sun in morning splendor mounts the sky;
Thy hopes, thy aims, thy destinies are high.
God make thee great, as thou art fair and free,
And give thee sons and daughters worthy thee,
O Canada, my country and my love.

Eternal blessing rest upon thy head!
Abounding Plenty heap thy board with bread!
Justice and Peace upon thy steps attend,
And Virtue be thy guardian and thy friend!
And Righteousness, like thine own maple tree,
Flourish and rear her shelter over thee,
O Canada, my country and my love.

SOL CANADIEN, TERRE CHERIE.

(From the French of Isidore Bedard.)

O soil Canadian, cherished earth

O soil Canadian, cherished earth,
The brave, the noble, peopled thee;
They left the country of their birth,
And sought a land of liberty.
It was from glorious France they came:
They were the pick of warriors, they;
The shining lustre of their fame
Is kept untarnished till to-day.

How beautiful thy fields appear!
How much thou hast to give content!
All hail, ye mountains that uprear
Your lordly heights magnificent!
All hail, St. Lawrence' noble tide!
Hail, land by Nature richly deckt!
Thy children's hearts should throb with pride,
Thy sons should walk with head erect.

Still honor the protecting hand
Of Albion, friend of the opprest;
And harbor no malicious band
Of traitors nourished in thy breast.
Yield never in the storm, be brave;
Thine only masters are thy laws;
Thou wast not made to be a slave;
Fear not, thy rights are Britain's cause.

If that belov'd, protecting hand
Should ever fail thee, undismay'd
Stand by thyself, alone, my land,
Rejecting, scorning foreign aid.
From glorious France thy founders came;
They were the pick of warriors, they:
The shining lustre of their fame
Unsullied shall be kept for aye.

MY OWN CANADIAN GIRL.

The demoiselles of sunny France

The demoiselles of sunny France
Have gaiety and grace;
Britannia's maids a tender glance,
A sweet and gentle face;
Columbia's virgins bring to knee
Full many a duke and earl;
But there is none can equal thee,
My own Canadian girl.

Thy hair is finer than the floss
That tufts the ears of corn;
Its tresses have a silken gloss,
A glory like the morn;
I prize the rich, luxuriant mass,
And each endearing curl
A special grace and beauty has,
My own Canadian girl.

Thy brow is like the silver moon
That sails in summer skies,
The mirror of a mind immune
From care, serene and wise,
Thy nose is sculptured ivory;
Thine ears are lobes of pearl;
Thy lips are corals from the sea,
My own Canadian girl.

Thine eyes are limpid pools of light,
The windows of thy soul;
The stars are not so clear and bright
That shine around the pole.
The crimson banners of thy cheeks
To sun and wind unfurl;
Thy tongue makes music when it speaks,
My own Canadian girl.

God keep thee fair and bright and good
As in thy morning hour,

And make thy gracious womanhood
A still unfolding flow'r.
And stay thy thoughts from trifles vain,
Thy feet from folly's whirl,
And guard thy life from every stain,
My own Canadian girl!

THE ST. LAWRENCE.

Though like Ulysses, fam'd of old

Though like Ulysses, fam'd of old,
I travell'd, or the wandering Jew,
No nobler sight could I behold
Than one which daily meets my view,
This mighty stream, my country's pride,
St. Lawrence' broad, majestic tide.

By Babylonia's waters, 'mong
Unwonted scenes, disconsolate,
Their harps upon the willows hung,
The Jewish exiles weeping sate,
Recall'd the river of their land,
And yearn'd to tread its winding strand.

When stern Elisha bade him lave
Seven times in Jordan and be clean,
His Syrian upland's flashing wave
Seem'd better to the Damascene.
"Albana, Pharpar far excel,"
He said, "the streams of Israel."

In India Ganges was rever'd,
In Egypt worshipp'd was the Nile,
To Romans Tiber was endear'd
From Apennine to Sacred Isle;
And Rhine and Danube, Thames and Rhone
A people's votive love have known.

And we to this imposing flood
A cordial homage needs must pay,
Who in the solemn night have stood
Upon its banks, and day by day
Been fill'd with gladness to behold
Its floor of silver flush'd with gold.

It brings the nations to our marts,
It bears our commerce to the sea,
Has virtue, too, to cleanse our hearts,
And make our spirits strong and free;

It flows, our struggling lives to bless,
With volume, grace and cheerfulness.

ST. LAWRENCE AND THE COMING SHIPS.

I cannot loiter on my way

I cannot loiter on my way,
The ice is drifting through Belle Isle,
And far to seaward by Cape Ray
Broad leagues of open water smile.
Unheeded now, the inland barge
Creeps heavily, the fisher dips
His meshes in my brimming marge;
I go to meet the coming ships.

They steam from Thames by Dover Strait,
They cleave the Bristol Channel's tide,
They pass the Mersey's thronging gate,
And issue from the crowded Clyde.
Out past the homing craft they sheer,
The Irish coastline by them slips;
Ere many days they will be here:
I go to meet the coming ships.

Full-fraught with wealth of merchandise,
They plough the main with furrows deep;
Upon the waves they sink and rise,
But onward, onward ever keep.
And some a viewless message send,
Whose airy flight their speed outstrips;
And all their yearnings hither tend:
I go to meet the coming ships.

I tarry not by fortress old,
Nor pause by any pleasant shore,
But hasten, eager to behold
Those brave leviathans once more,
To welcome them with parted banks,
And kiss their prows with loving lips,
And soothingly caress their flanks;
I go to meet the coming ships.

THE QUEBEC EXODUS.

Why should we leave the soil our fathers cleared

Why should we leave the soil our fathers cleared,
And lifelong tilled with patient, loving hands?
Why should we leave the homes our fathers reared,
And seek strange dwellings in unhallowed lands?
Why should we leave the shrines where they revered
Their guardian God, and break the golden bands
That bind us to the ashes of our sires,
Their haunts, their hearthstones and their altar-fires?

Is it that now no longer from our doors
The forest stretches with its gloom profound?
That they who first set foot upon these shores
Increase and multiply and hedge us round,
Co-heritors of the exhaustless stores
Of natural wealth that more and more abound?—
Because of brethren of a differing speech,
From whom we learn, and whom perhaps we teach?

It was not thus our conquering race arose;
It was not thus our copious language grew:
The Saxon mingled with his Celtic foes,
The Norman brought to both a spirit new.
Not thus we read th' heroic tale of those
Who built the younger Britains o'er the blue:
'Twas here and there a handful in the earth,
Prevailing, not by numbers, but by worth.

HEAT.

The fickle sun that had the earth caress'd

The fickle sun that had the earth caress'd
And quickened all her amorous desire,
And brought fresh roses to adorn her breast,
Now spurned her in the madness of his ire;
A haze of heat half hid the mountain's crest;
The very river seemed of liquid fire;
The air was flame, the town a stifling pale,
And all the land was like a Hinnom's Vale.

I thought of Hagar and what she endured,
Faint in the desert, driv'n from Sara's sight;
Of angry Jonah underneath his gourd,
Grown in a night and withered in a night;
Of the sun-stricken lad Elisha cured
For the good, hospitable Shunammite;
And of the fiery furnace made to glow
For Shadrach, Meshach and Abednego.

I called to mind Boccaccio's tale of her
Left on a sun-scorched roof, and like to die;
And I beheld the Ancient Mariner
Becalmed beneath his hot and copper sky;
And heard a long-forgotten traveller
Speak from a page which made my childhood sigh,
And tell of horrid climes by God accurst,
And men and horses perishing of thirst.

And to myself I said, Is this the land
Where freezing cold claims sometimes half the year?
Is this the region where the streams are spanned
With floors of azure crystal, hard and clear,
And all the snow-enveloped mountains stand
Like hoary chiefs, majestic and austere?
Was't here we saw so late King Winter stern?
And will he shortly here again return?

INVOCATION TO SUMMER.

Come, Summer, come, nor in the south delay

Come, Summer, come, nor in the south delay;
We do thee honor with a longer day;
We prize thee more, we better know thy worth;
We hold thee dearer in the truer north:
Come, Summer, come.

Come, Summer, come, and in the early dawn
Find sparkling dewdrops on the fragrant lawn;
Hush all before thy majesty at noon,
And hallow the long evening hours; come soon,
Come, Summer, come.

Come, Summer, come, make meadow grasses long;
Make all the groves exuberant with song,
The pasture corners canopy with shades,
And thickly roof the silent forest glades:
Come, Summer, come.

Come, Summer, come, and with thy magic breath
Make consummation of the death of death;
Complete the work of thy sweet sister, Spring;
Life more abundantly give everything:
Come, Summer, come.

SIR SUMMER.

When conquering Summer stalks the street

When conquering Summer stalks the street,
His eyes are eyes of fire,
The pavement burns beneath his feet,
Men droop before his ire;
But yonder, out upon the land,
His manners are not these:
He is a courtier mild and bland
Beneath the maple trees.

He throws his buckler on the grass,
Unclasps his sheathèd blade;
He doffs his helmet and cuirass,
And lounges in the shade;
His pennon, fastened to a bough,
Is fluttering in the breeze:
He is at home and happy now
Beneath the maple trees.

No furious rage disturbs his breast,
No fever heats his brain;
Right cheerily he takes his rest,
And views his glad domain;
His lady seated by his side,
His children on his knees,
His heart expands with joy and pride
Beneath the maple trees.

He hears the happy farmer folk
Who toss the fragrant hay;
Blessings upon him they invoke,
And beg of him to stay.
The music of the feathered choirs,
The murmur of the bees,
Are sounds of which he never tires
Beneath the maple trees.

He hums a sweet, melodious tune,
His hand a garland weaves,

He talks the while he feasts at noon,
His laughter shakes the leaves.
He tells of conquests in the south,
Of triumphs overseas,
Of realms redeemed and deeds of drouth,
Beneath the maple trees.

He shouts and holds his jolly sides,
And strikes his lusty thigh,
To think of how Sir Winter hides
His face when he is nigh,
Or how with city exquisites
His swagger disagrees:
Thus glad Sir Summer gaily sits
Beneath the maple trees.

I know where I can find his bower
Upon a wooded hill,
Where I can pluck his favorite flower,
And bathe within his rill;
And thither I will take my flight,
And loiter at my ease,
And pay my homage to the Knight
Beneath the maple trees.

THE NIGHT.

A tremor, a quiver, through her ran

A tremor, a quiver,
Through her ran
As over the river
The dawn began.
She drew her veil
Over her eyes,
And her face grew pale,
As she watched the sun rise.
She faded, turned
To a ghost, was gone,
As the morning burned
And the day came on.
With veiled, sad eye,
And face still wan,
She waited nigh
When the dusk began.
With her tears of bliss
The earth was wet,
And soothed with her kiss,
When the sun had set.
And with stately pride
She sat on the throne
Of her empire wide
When the day had gone;
And her robes she spread
With their sable hem,
And crowned her head
With her diadem.
And the mute earth saw
That a Queen was she,
And gazed with awe
On her majesty.

TO BEAUTY.

Beauty, beloved of all gentle hearts

Beauty, beloved of all gentle hearts
And pure, and cherished of the gifted tribe
Whose skill to canvas and even stone imparts
Such things as words are powerless to describe.
And bards, who woo thee in the silent shade
And dote upon thee under moonlit skies,
And lovers, who behold thee new-array'd,
As our first parents did in Paradise!

These all have been thy priests. In times remote,
In Athens and the cool Thessalian dells,
They sung thy liturgy with dulcet note,
And quaff'd thy chalice from the sacred wells
Of leafy Helicon. Beneath the brows
Of fam'd Olympus and among the isles
Of the Aegean sea they paid their vows,
And read thy lore in Nature's frowns and smiles.

Nor strange to Zion's sanctuaried hill
Wast thou, embalmer of the holy page;
Ambrosial odors from thy garments fill
The garden where the amorous royal sage
Walk'd and discours'd with his beloved; there
Alluring in thy soft and sumptuous dress:
And to his kinglier sire supremely fair,
Companion sweet of meek-ey'd Holiness.

Thou hast no local temple, no set shrine;
Thou art diffus'd o'er earth and sky and sea;
In every land a thousand haunts are thine,
Spirits of every race respond to thee.
Here thy Olympus and thy Zion hill,
Thy silvery Aegean, I survey;
Thy majesty and loveliness at will
I view, and own thy tranquilizing sway.

THE DOCTOR.

He bent above our darling's bed

He bent above our darling's bed
When her life was ebbing low,
And in his serious look we read
The truth we feared to know.

We knew a slender thread was all
That held her now; we saw
The dark, portentous shadow fall,
And near and nearer draw.

Our hopes were centred all in him;
We stood with bated breath
As, pitiful and calm and grim,
He fought and fought with Death.

We hung upon the desperate fight,
And saw in him combined
The tiger's stealth, the lion's might,
The man's superior mind.

We saw the fearful hate he bore
His old, relentless foe,
His beautiful compassion for
The one we cherished so.

No mortal ever waged alone
A conflict so severe;
The high-souled, stainless champion
Finds heavenly succor near.

Legions of angels to his aid
His pure devotion brought;
Celestial strength his spirit swayed;
'Twas Life that in him fought.

The awful stillness of the night!
The long and bitter hours!—
It seemed that Time had stayed his flight
To watch the battling pow'rs.

And ere the ghastly night had fled

He conquered in the strife,
And gently took the slender thread,
And drew her back to life.

MY VALENTINE.

O Dorothy, sweet Dorothy

O Dorothy, sweet Dorothy,
You make my heart rejoice;
Your presence is like Arcady,
There's music in your voice;
Heaven's purity is on your brow,
Its light is in your eyne;
I love you, and I ask you now
To be my Valentine.

Your face is like the lily in
The morning's ruddy light;
Your dimpled cheeks and tiny chin
Are blessings to my sight;
Your lips are fairer than the rose
And redder far than wine;
Your teeth are whiter than the snows:
You'll be my Valentine!

You are not quite so old as I,
You've seen but summers three;
And that's no doubt the reason why
You are not coy with me.
I'll come to you to-morrow,
And on chocolates we'll dine;
And you'll have no thought of sorrow
When you are my Valentine.

MY FRIENDS.

Some to and fro for converse flit

My never-failing friends are they,
With whom I converse day by day." — *Southey.*

Some to and fro for converse flit
And on their friends intrude,
Or shun society and sit
In cheerless solitude;
But I can sit, when night descends,
At home among a thousand friends.

The garish day is left behind,
The scurry and the din;
The hours of toil are out of mind,
As if they had not been.
No thought of morrow that impends
Comes in between me and my friends.

We reck not of the flight of time,
To them a subject strange;
They pass their days in a sublime
Indifference to change:
Theirs is the life that never ends;
Immortal beings are my friends.

They toil not, neither do they spin;
Yet none is meanly drest;
And some are clad in costly skin,
And some in silken vest;
And everyone who sees commends
The decent habits of my friends.

And some are short, and some are tall;
Some portly, and some spare;
Here is a group of pygmies small,
A Tom Thumb family; there
A Brobdingnagian row extends,
The best-informed among my friends.

Wot one among them all is low,

A fellow to be spurned;
And none is ever rude, although
Their backs are often turned.
No observation that offends
Is dropped by any of my friends.

And some are steeped in classic lore;
Some brim with wisdom sage;
And some can trace a far-off shore,
Or paint a former age;
And each his talent freely lends,
For talented are all my friends.

Some tell of deeds and lives sublime
And triumphs over foes;
Some weave a spell of lofty rhyme,
Some charm with stately prose;
And here and there a mind unbends
Familiarly among my friends.

In diction antiquated, quaint,
Or with a modern sound,
They speak their thoughts without restraint,
Although they're mostly bound;
And cease to speak when none attends,
A valued feature of my friends.

Although they shun the thoughtless crowd,
The frivolous disdain,
Their titles have not made them proud,
Nor all their pages vain;
No common mortal less pretends,
None can be opener than my friends.

They care not that they've all been cut,
A number by myself,
And often taken down, and put
As often on the shelf;
My estimation makes amends
For such ill-treatment of my friends.

An ever-fresh, unfailing source
Of thought and sympathy,
What hours of goodly intercourse
They have afforded me!
I cannot doubt that heaven still sends
Us angels while I have my friends.

If he who sits at home in gloom,
Or rushes here and there,
Will put a bookshelf in his room

And furnish it with care,
He'll bless the evenings that he spends
With such companions as my friends.

NOTHING TOO GOOD FOR THE IRISH.

It's the Emerald Isle is the beautiful land

It's the Emerald Isle is the beautiful land:
There's nothing too good for the Irish.
O'er the whole of it, Nature, at heaven's command,
Has scattered her charms with a prodigal hand
From Skibbereen town to the Donegal strand;
For there's nothing too good for the Irish.

And it's many a hero the Irish can claim:
There's nothing too good for the Irish.
"Red Hugh" put his country's invaders to shame;
Owen Roe was a fighter they never could tame;
As a nation the Irish have glory and fame;
For there's nothing too good for the Irish.

And the Irish are noted for piety, too:
There's nothing too good for the Irish.
In the far-away time before Brian Boru,
The faith by Saint Patrick was planted and grew,
And the "Island of Saints" has had saints not a few:
For there's nothing too good for the Irish.

And the best of all orators Irishmen are:
There's nothing too good for the Irish.
The voice of Columba was heard from afar,
Burke's eloquence rolled like a conquering car,
And the name of O'Connell's a radiant star;
For there's nothing too good for the Irish.

And the Irishman always is witty, of course;
There's nothing too good for the Irish.
And his wit is as genial and kind as its source;
It never leaves anyone feeling the worse;
He makes bulls, but a good Irish bull's a white horse;
For there's nothing too good for the Irish.

You are thinking, no doubt, to the race I belong:
There's nothing too good for the Irish.
You think I am Irish, but that's where you're wrong;
I am Scotch, but our love for the Irish is strong;

We gave them a saint and we'll give them a song;
For there's nothing too good for the Irish.

AN ENGLISH TOAST.

The English soil!—'tis hallowed ground

The English soil!—'tis hallowed ground:
Its restless children roam
The world, but they have never found
So dear a land as home;
Their passion for its hills and downs
Nor space nor time can spoil;
A golden mist of memory crowns
The good old English soil.

The English race!—its pluck and pith,
Its power to stay and win,—
Wise Alfred's, dauntless Harold's kith,
And Coeur de Lion's kin!
Sir Philip Sidney, Hampden, Noll,
Who sat in kingly place!
Wolfe, Nelson, Wellington and all
The good old English race!

The English speech!—the copious tongue,
Terse, vivid, plastic, fit,
Which Chaucer, Spenser loved and sung,
Which gave us Holy Writ;
Which Shakespeare, Milton used, to write,
Which Taylor used, to preach,
And Pitt, to speak, as we to-night—
The good old English speech!

"St. George and Merrie England!"—still
The stirring phrase imparts
Warmth to the blood, and sends a thrill
Through more than English hearts.
God save Old England by His grace!
We all alike beseech,
Who know the English soil or race
And speak the English speech.

THE SCOT.

That no Scotsman is perfect, we freely confess

That no Scotsman is perfect, we freely confess,
Nor has been since the time of the fall;
Yet we think, notwithstanding and nevertheless,
He is "nae sheep-shank bane," after all.
"Sic excellent pairts" as he has will atone
For the lack of a tittle or jot;
And, although we don't boast, it is very well known
For some things you must go to a Scot.

If you want a sweet song that comes straight from the heart
Of a man who had few for his peers,
An approved son of genius and master of art.
And a lover, with laughter and tears;
A song that gives honor to personal worth,
And ennobles the lowliest lot,
And makes brothers of all who inhabit the earth;
You must go "for a' that" to a Scot.

If you want a good story, entrancingly told,
By a genuine king of the pen,
A right royal dispenser of things new and old,
And a faithful portrayer of men;
A tale that will brighten your work and your play,
And will do what some others do not,—
Give you knowledge and wisdom and heart for the fray;
You will go to Sir Walter, the Scot.

If you want the high spirit that scorns to make truce
With a foeman on suppliant knee,
The untameable will of a Wallace or Bruce,
Or the dash of a Bonnie Dundee;
Fierce courage that nothing on earth can subdue,
Sense of honor that shrinks from a blot,
Inexhaustible loyalty, loving and true,
You will find them to-day in a Scot.

If you want an intense love of country and kin,
An attachment as tender as strong,

That can gar the blood leap when the pipers begin,
And the tear start at sound of a song;
A grand patriotic devotion and pride,
That makes sanctified ground of the spot
Where a Scotsman for freedom has suffered and died;
You will find what you want in a Scot.

If you want a hale-bodied and clear-headed chiel,
Independent and honest and good,
With a hand that can do and a heart that can feel,
And tenacious of purpose—and shrewd;
Whose thrift makes the face of prosperity smile,
Who's contented with what he has got,
But is ready and careful to add to his pile;
You may find what you want in a Scot.

Gin ye wush a douce body, auldfarrant and gash,
Unco' waukrife and couthie and braw,
Ower eydent wi' daft clishmaclavers to fash,
Or to thole whigmaleeries ava;
Mak's nae collieshangie wad fley a bit flee,
But is siccer and dour as a stot;
Tak's the scone and the kebbuck and carries the gree;
Ye'll be spierin', gude faith! for a Scot.

GLOSSARY.—"Nae sheep-shank bane" (Burns), no unimportant person; "gars," makes; "chiel," fellow; "gin," if; "wush," wish; "douce," sober; "auldfarrant," wise; "gash," sagacious; "unco," uncommonly; "waukrife," wideawake; "couthie," kindly; "braw," handsome; "ower," over; "eydent," busy; "daft," foolish; "clishmaclavers," idle talk; "fash," trouble; "thole," bear; "whigmaleeries," crotchets; "ava," at all; "collieshangie," commotion; "fley," disturb; "siccer," steady; "dour," stubborn; "stot," ox; "scone," a cake; "kebbuck," a cheese; "carries the gree" (Burns), has the pre-eminence; "spierin'," inquiring.

THE ROARIN' GAME.

The roarin' game, the roarin' game

The roarin' game, the roarin' game,
From Scotland's bonnie land it came,
The land of loch and firth and ben,
And comely dames and stalwart men;
It crossed the broad Atlantic tide
With Scots who came to dwell this side,
And bring our country wealth and fame,
The roarin' game, the roarin' game.

The roarin' game, the roarin' game
Makes every land to Scotsmen "hame";
Where'er the winter's breath congeals
The water, see the sturdy "chiels"
With "stane" and besom play and sweep,
Intently gaze, and shout and leap,
With genial fervor all aflame:—
The roarin' game, the roarin' game.

The roarin' game, the roarin' game,
Though stupid folk may think it tame,
Affect the smile that wisdom casts
On rattle-brained enthusiasts,
And jest in condescending tones
Of boys and marbles, men and stones;
'Tis fine enjoyment just the same,
The roarin' game, the roarin' game.

The roarin' game, the roarin' game
Its meed of praise may justly claim:
As firm as ice upon the pond
It is of hearts a brother bond;
It trains us to be wise and true
In all we undertake to do,
And fits for every higher aim,
The roarin' game, the roarin' game.

The roarin' game, the roarin' game
Will never give us cause for shame,

No shattered nerves and aching heads,
Bad consciences and nameless dreads,
But health and strength and minds serene
And kindly hearts and friendly mien:
No honest tongue will e'er defame
The roarin' game, the roarin' game.

THE OLD SCOTTISH MINISTER.

A man he was of Scottish race

A man he was of Scottish race,
And ancient Scottish name;
Of common mould, but lofty mien,
That dignified his frame.
And he lived a humble, quiet life,
Obscure, unknown to fame;
God's glory and the good of man
His constant, only aim:
Like a fine old Scottish minister,
All of the olden time.

He dearly loved his gentle wife,
As everyone could tell;
And watched his children as they grew,
Lest any ill befell;
And as he looked upon his boys
His bosom oft would swell;
For he reared them in the fear of God,
And ruled his household well:
Like a true old Scottish minister,
All of the olden time.

A father, too, he was to all
His congregation there:
To all he felt a father's love,
And showed a father's care:
He wisely counselled them with speech,
And pled for them in prayer;
And ever for the needy ones
He something had to spare:
Like a kind old Scottish minister,
All of the olden time.

The servant of the Lord he was,
In hovel and in hall,—
The high ambassador of heaven
Whom earth could not enthrall;
Like Christ among the wedding guests,

Or by the funeral pall;
And he made his daily life sublime,
A pattern unto all:
Like a grand old Scottish minister,
All of the olden time.

For truth and righteousness and love
His voice was ever heard;
And minds were kindled into thought,
And consciences were stirred,
And weary, heavy-laden hearts
To faith and hope were spurred,
As from the pulpit he proclaimed
The everlasting Word:
Like a faithful Scottish minister,
All of the olden time.

And when, amid his elders grave,
Extended in a line
Beside the table of the Lord,
He kept the rite divine,
His face with a rapt, unearthly look
Was seen to strangely shine,
As he broke the white, symbolic bread,
And passed the sacred wine:
Like a saintly Scottish minister,
All of the olden time.

His lot was hard, his task severe;
He found the burden light:
When darkly o'er his pathway hung
The shadows of the night,
His heart was steadfast, for he walked
By faith, and not by sight;
And ran triumphantly his course,
And fought a goodly fight:
Like a brave old Scottish minister,
All of the olden time.

And when upon a summer's day
He laid him down to die,
He called his household to his side
Without a moan or sigh,
And blessed his children each in turn,
And said a fond good-bye,
And then consigned his soul to God,
And went to live on high:
Like a good old Scottish minister,
All of the olden time.

THE MACS.

There's a race, or a part of a race, if you will

There's a race, or a part of a race, if you will,
Of renown prehistoric, and vigorous still,
Who back from their fastnesses scornfully hurl'd
The redoubtable legions that trampled the world;
They repelled, and they only, the Roman attacks,
The stalwart, courageous, impetuous Macs.

When the red-bearded pirates, the Saxons and Danes
And Angles, came swarming across the sea plains,
And the old British stock to exterminate tried,
Caledonia and Erin their efforts defied;
And the conquering Normans were glad to make tracks
From the Macs and the Mics (who are properly Macs).

Their proud patronymics, they rightfully hold,
Proclaim them descended from heroes of old.—
Illustrious titles that throw in the shade
The dukedoms and earldoms but yesterday made;
And even the King with his royalty lacks
A lineage as ancient as that of the Macs.

They are old and yet young, with a spirit possest
By the dream of the East and the hope of the West;
The earth is their country, the race is their kin;
In populous cities their guerdon they win,
And in gold miners' cabins and lumbermen's shacks
You will find the ubiquitous, venturesome Macs.

Distinguished they've been with the sword and the pen;
In pulpit and parliament, leaders of men;
Prime ministers, presidents, merchants, viziers,
They have manag'd the business of both hemispheres;
And the Dago day-laborers laying the tracks
Are boss'd by the Macs or the Mics (who are Macs).

'Twas thought by the ancients that Atlas upbore
The sphere on his shoulders—'tis thought so no more;
Prometheus and Atlas and all of their kith,
The Titans, are now but a fable, a myth.

The men who are bearing the world on their backs
Are the Macs and the Mics (who are mixed with the Macs).

THE PARSON AT THE HOCKEY MATCH.

It's very disagreeable to sit here in the cold

It's very disagreeable to sit here in the cold,
And a sinful waste of time—ah, well, it's too late now to scold;
I'll think about my sermon and my prayers for Sunday next,
And the young folks may be happy—let me see—what was my text?
But what a throng of people—an immortal soul in each:
With such an audience this would be a splendid place to preach.
I'd have the pulpit half-way down—what ice! without a smirch!
Here are the men—I wonder if they ever go to church.
"The teams?" Ah, yes, "the forwards, point, and cover-point and goal";
Thank you, my dear, I understand—is that a lump of coal?
"Rubber?" Ah, yes, "The puck?" just so! One's holding it, I see—
That fellow with his clothes all on—ah, that's the referee.
What was he whistling for—his dog? Why, they've begun to play;
Well, well, that's rough; I really think we're doing wrong to stay.
It's sickening, deafening; dear! I wish this uproar could be stilled.
I do sincerely trust there'll not be anybody killed.

It's a wondrous exhibition of alertness, speed, and strength.
I suppose there's not much danger—there's a fellow at full length.
He's up again; that's plucky. Well, the little lad has pluck—
And now he's master of the ice, possessor of the puck.
He dodges two opponents, but collides with one at last,
A Philistine Goliath—David baffles him and fast
Darts onward o'er the whitening sheet, while from each crowded row
The crazed spectators cheer him on—Look!—has he lost it? No!
He's clear again. Played, played, my boy. I'd like to see him score:—
(I'll have no voice for Sunday if I shout like this much more)—
But there his ruthless enemies o'erwhelm him in a shoal—
Well played, you hero, safely passed. Now for a shot on goal.
Shoot, shoot, you duffer; shoot, you goose, you ass, you great galoot,
You addle-pated idiot, you nincompoop, you—shoot!
You've lost it! Never mind—well tried—that other dash was grand.
Why do they stop? "Off side," you say? I don't quite understand.
That's puzzling. I suppose it's right. I wish they'd not delay.
This is a most provoking interruption to the play.

"Cold?" Nothing of the sort. I was—I'm heated with the game.

I'm really enjoying it; indeed, I'm glad I came.
I'd like to see both ends at once; I can't from where we sit.
They've scored one yonder—What's the row? A player has been hit?
Such things are bound to happen in a rapid game like this;
They'll soon resume the play, my dear; there's nothing much amiss,—
Some trifling accident received in a rough body check,
A shoulder dislocated or a fracture of the neck.
Oh, no, it's nothing serious—the game begins again.
They're here, a writhing, struggling mass of half a dozen men
Battling and groaning with the strife, and breathing hard and fast,
Swayed back and forth and stooping low like elms before the blast,
Changing their places like a fleet of vessels tempest-driven
That blindly meet within the waves and part with timbers riven,
Waving their sticks with frantic zeal—But isn't this a sight?
My goodness! I could sit and watch a game like this all night.
There, dirty trousers, there's your chance. Muffed it! Why weren't you quick?
This is a sight to make the sad rejoice, to heal the sick,
To rouse the drones and give them life to last them half a year—
Hit him again!—I wish I had my congregation here.

My stars! and this is hockey. Hockey's the king of sports.
This is the thing to come to when you're feeling out of sorts.
This is the greatest holiday I've had for many weeks.
This helps one to appreciate the feeling of the Greeks.
I understand my Homer now—O Hercules, behold
Yon Trojan giant, he that's cast in an Olympian mould,
Ye gods, he more than doubled up that other stalwart cove—
Here comes swift-footed Mercury, the messenger of Jove.
Adown the blue, outstripping all, he speeds. Oh, what a spurt!
His shoulders have no wings, but see, he has them on his shirt.
He's broken through the forward line, baffled the cover-point,
Thrown down the other man and knocked their game all out of joint.
And now he rushes on the goal—this makes the senses reel—
Goal! goal! hurrah! hurrah! well done, men of the winged wheel!

At last—how soon!—the game is done; I've scarcely drawn a breath.
This getting out is difficult; I'm almost crushed to death.
The cars are packed; how we'll get home I'm sure I do not know.
Here's room for you; get up, my dears; I'll walk; away you go.

My sermon's gone, but as I walk I cannot help but think
That, after all, perhaps I've found a sermon in the rink.

This world is an arena with a slippery sheet of ice,
And all have skates and hockey sticks and enter without price.
And seats are round for those who rest—the idle and the old;
But those who are not in the game are apt to find it cold.
Some play defence, some forward, with terrific speed and stress.
The puck keeps flying 'twixt the goals of failure and success,

Now up, now down, across and back, here, there, and everywhere.

The grit of skates, the crack of sticks, the shouting, fill the air.
Some slip and fall a thousand times and spring up in a trice;
Some go to pieces on their feet and have to leave the ice;
Some play offside, kick, tackle, trip, try every kind of foul;
Some players are forever cheered, some only get a howl.
We seldom hear the whistle of the watchful Referee,
Who mostly lets the game go on as if He didn't see.
No gong rings out half-time to let the players get their breath—
To most full time comes only with the solemn stroke of death.
The winners are not always those who make the biggest score:
The vanquished oft are victors when the stubborn game is o'er;
For many things are added to make up the grand amount,
And everything is taken at the last into account—
The sort of sticks we played with, and the way our feet were shod,
For the trophy is Salvation and the Referee is God.

God prosper our Canadian sports and keep them clean and pure,
Whole-hearted, manly, generous, and let them long endure!
Long live each honest winter sport, each good Canadian game,
To train the youth in lusty health and iron strength of frame,
To make them noble, vigorous, straightforward, ardent, bold,
Nearer a perfect standard than the grandest knights of old.

Keep in the path of rectitude the young throughout the land,
And guide them ever on their way by thine unerring hand,
Along the slippery path of life in safety toward the goal,
And keep their bodies holy as the temples of the soul:
For the river of the future from the present's fountain runs,
And a nation's hope is founded on the virtue of her sons.

The glory of a man is strength, Thy wisdom hath declared:
Let strength increase, and strength of frame with strength of will be paired,
And let these twain go hand in hand with strength of heart and mind,
And strength of character present all forms of strength combined.
Oh, make out strength the strength of men to perfect stature grown,
And use it for thine ends and turn man's glory to thine own.

Lector House believes that a society develops through a two-fold approach of continuous learning and adaptation, which is derived from the study of classic literary works spread across the historic timeline of literature records. Therefore, we aim at reviving, repairing and redeveloping all those inaccessible or damaged but historically as well as culturally important literature across subjects so that the future generations may have an opportunity to study and learn from past works to embark upon a journey of creating a better future.

This book is a result of an effort made by Lector House towards making a contribution to the preservation and repair of original ancient works which might hold historical significance to the approach of continuous learning across subjects.

HAPPY READING & LEARNING!

LECTOR HOUSE

LECTOR HOUSE LLP

E-MAIL: info@lectorhouse.com

9 789356 146112

9 789356 146112

Printed by Libri Plureos GmbH in Hamburg, Germany